Never underestimate
the power you have
to change your world

Categories?

Let's start by imagining our nation
the day after the election.
Half the people party;
their candidate won.
The other half mourn;
their candidate lost.

Is this what we want?
Do we really want to divide our nation
into winners and losers?
Do we really want to force others
to lose
so we can win?
Is that who we are?

I don't think so.

Let's imagine a different outcome.
The election is over,
and everyone is happy,
because every voter wins.

Impossible?
Maybe.
But then again,
maybe not.

It all depends
on whether we're willing to think
outside the box.

What if we woke up tomorrow
and there were no political parties?
No Democrat.
No Republican.
No red state.
No blue state.
No liberal.
No conservative.
What if we were all just people?

What would we discover
about one another?

Suppose we could reboot
without all the baggage in our brains.
Who knows?
We might actually like each other.

Maybe we aren't as far apart
as we think we are.

Three hundred million people
call America home.
There's something wrong with a system
where a presidential election
becomes a choice
of the lesser of two evils.
Instead, it should be
a tough choice
among our favorite leaders.
We should want
to vote for everybody
on the ballot.

Where are those candidates?
Why can't we find them?
And how did we create a system
that divides the country
into winners and losers every election day?
Why can't we all be winners?

Right now, when someone gets elected,
half the country parties
while the other half feels
as though doom itself has fallen
upon our nation.
Whoa!
We gotta find a better way
of coming to a consensus than that.
Elections are not wars
that are won or lost.
Elections should be opportunities
for all of us to be heard
and every person to be validated.

It's possible
you know.

We just need to change
the way we think.

And we need to find a way
to listen.

Every person has a story.
What would happen
if we listened
to those stories?

What would we discover?

Suppose we listened
to the quiet people
who don't do bumper stickers
or political posts on Facebook
but have much to add
to the conversation.

What if we welcomed them
into the conversation?
What if we gave them
a voice?

The way we have the conversation
is just as important
as the point
we want to make.

The louder one talks
the less we hear.

If we don't care about each other,
we cannot have a conversation.
If we don't respect one another,
we cannot have a conversation.
If we won't understand each other,
we cannot have a conversation.
If we don't trust one another,
we cannot have a conversation.

Political debate
without care
without respect
without understanding
without trust
is pointless.
It gets us nowhere.

Change the culture first;
politics will follow.

Suppose you and I
were locked in a prison cell, and
we had three days to learn
how to understand,
care about,
trust and
respect each other.
If we succeed,
the door opens
and we walk into heaven.
If we fail,
the floor vanishes,
and we fall into hell.
Could we do it?
Would we do it?

Don't we create
our own heaven or hell
here on earth
by the way we treat one another?

The campus protests of the 1960s
need not set the tone
for national dialogue today.
We went through a troubled time.
But we grew up.
Standing across from each other
and shouting
is so *yesterday*.
Couldn't we sit down,
invite one another to pull up a chair,
share a cup of coffee,
and listen?

What I'm talking about here
is a change in mindset.
Instead of pointing in every direction
and finding enemies,
let's look around
and find friends.

Some say
we must compromise.

I'm not so sure.
When we compromise,
don't we both lose
something?
Doesn't everybody feel
just a little bit cheated?

What if we kept talking
and listening
and thinking
until we came up with
a creative alternative
that everyone likes.

We can do that
you know
if we stop caring
who gets the credit,
who gets to be in charge,
and what's in it for me.
Instead, we focus our care
on what's best for everybody.

If everybody
wants what's best
for everybody,
then everybody
wins.

What if
we changed the way
we elect our president
and our other political leaders?

Suppose
instead of two political parties
at war with one another,
we identified leaders
who want the best
for everybody.

What if,
in the case of
a Presidential election,
we narrowed it down
to the ten leaders
America likes the best?

At the voting booth
you get to rank them:
your first choice,
your second choice,
and so on,
for as many as you wish to vote for.

If your first choice doesn't get enough votes
then your vote gets transferred
to your second choice
and so on.

In this way,
almost everybody
wins.

When the constitution was written,
we didn't have the technology to do that.

Now we do.

This system—
sometimes called
ranked choice voting,
instant-runoff voting
transferable voting,
or preferential voting—
may also help us decide critical issues
where every American
should have a voice.[1]

---

1   For more information, see
     http://youtu.be/s7tWHJfhiyo,
     http://youtu.be/3Y3jE3B8HsE,
     http://youtu.be/l8XOZJkozfI

I'm not a Democrat,
and I'm not a Republican.
I'm not conservative,
I'm not liberal,
and I'm not centrist.
I don't do categories.
Categories divide.
Leaders unite.

You're you.
I'm me.
If we listen to each other long enough,
we'll discover
what we have in common
is far more important
than what we don't.

Seesawing back and forth
between Democrats and Republicans
does nothing to move our country forward.
All it does
is pit one half the country
against the other half.
If the only way to win
is to make half the country lose,
have we really won?
As Jim Rohn once said,
"There's just one problem
with trying to sink half the ship …
guess what happens to your half."
Leadership moves the country forward—
leaders who care about all the people,
not just the ones who vote for them.

What if we stopped keeping score?
Who cares
whether a solution
is a Democrat idea
or a Republican idea
or a Libertarian idea
or whatever?
What if public servants
stopped serving a political party
and just served the public?

*Thinking
outside the box*

The health of a nation
is determined
by how those who have power
treat those who have none.

I dream of a nation
where the rich,
the poor,
and the middle class
take the time to listen to one another,
understand one another
and learn from one another.

Don't underestimate
what the poor have to offer.
Their life experiences
give them perspective
that a middle class or rich person
may never have.

Some people want to

stick it to the rich.

But, hey,
if we got honest,
wouldn't all of us like to be rich?

I dream of a nation
where we're honest enough to admit
that something isn't working
and brave enough
to try something else.

For example,
our war on poverty—
how are we doing?

Not so good.

The government gives out welfare benefits.
For some, this is a life saver—literally.
For others,
this is the cause of great resentment.
They believe their hard work
is going to prop up
those who are too lazy to work.
Is that belief true and accurate?
Maybe not,
but one thing is clear:
The current system
is not getting people out of poverty.

We've created a system
where welfare workers
have zero motivation
to lift their clients out of poverty.
If they do,
they get lifted
right out of a job.
In addition,
for many people on welfare,
making more money
actually lowers their standard of living
because of the loss of food stamps,
earned income credit,
health care benefits,
Pell Grants
and so on.
Instead of ridding ourselves of poverty,
we've erected a wall around poverty
that keeps people in
who want to get out.
The harder they work,
the less money they have.

Would you work overtime
in order to get a smaller paycheck?
Would you double your hours at work
in order to get half a paycheck?

Think about that.
For a middle class or rich person
the harder you work,
the more money you have.
But for many poor people,
the harder they work,
the less money they have.

How do we solve this?
We begin with respect.
People in poverty deserve
to be treated with respect
just like anybody else.
They need to be listened to.
Their voices need to be heard.
They have something of value
to offer.

Why would we assume
that just because people are poor
they don't have anything to teach us?

In the process of listening,
I think we'll discover
one size does NOT fit all
when it comes to lifting people
out of poverty.
Every family is different,
and the needs of each individual
should be taken into account.

Before you turn the page,
I need to ask:
Are you willing to think
outside the box?

Consider this:
Who knows the most
about making money—
the rich,
the poor,
or the middle class?

What if it was in the financial interest
of the rich
to teach the poor
how to make money?

What if, for example,
a rich person got a tax rebate
for every family s/he lifts out of poverty?
Doesn't that make more sense
than the government spending all its money
trying to prevent welfare fraud?

Suppose each rich person
is responsible
for a certain number of poor families.
If that rich person can find a way
to lift these families out of poverty,
then he gets to keep the money
that he would otherwise spend on relief
for these poor families.

Suppose rich people
form cooperatives to do this.
These cooperatives will find solutions
that really work
to help people escape poverty.
For the rich,
it's just another investment.
For the poor,
it's freedom.

I'm just thinking outside the box here.
What if we all did that?

You may have a much better idea
than I do.
And that's cool.
In fact,
that's fantastic.

And, hey,
let's get together
and remove the shackles
that keep people
locked in poverty.

What if we put our heads together
and came up with ideas
we can test
small scale?
If they work,
scale up.
If they don't,
back to the drawing board.

Let's not be afraid
to fund things that work,
and dump the programs that don't.

Here's another thought:

Suppose the government
got out of the taxation business altogether.
What if the government
was forced to find a way
to finance its operations
without collecting a cent in taxes?
Are we smart enough to figure that out?
I say it can be done,
if we want it bad enough.

Hint:
How do people make money?

Sometimes you gotta put away
your prejudices
and think outside the box.

What if every family
were energy independent?
What if the grid
was a back up plan
rather than our only plan?

Why would we buy our energy
from people who hate us?
Why make them rich at our expense?

Couldn't we work
toward energy independence?
Couldn't we also work
toward green clean energy?
Aren't both important?

Just thinking out loud.

Dreams

We all have dreams.

If I tell you some of my dreams,
would you be willing
to tell me some of yours?

I dream of a world where any person
of any age,
gender,
race
or religion
can walk down any street
in any neighborhood
at any time
and be perfectly safe.

In more than fifty nations
around the world
it is dangerous and/or illegal
to be a Christian.

This is nothing new.
It has been going on
for twenty centuries.

But left unchecked,
it will find its way
to your neighborhood.
Don't think it won't affect you.
When corrupt governments
or militant groups
finish wiping out Christians,
you could be
next on their hit list.

That's why
I dream of a world
where everyone is free
to follow his or her conscience,
and where everyone
shows courtesy and consideration
for others
as they exercise that freedom.

I dream of a world
where everyone is equally free
to voice an opinion
on anything,
and no one need fear
repercussions
for doing so.

I dream of a world
where every child has a daddy
who stays,
who cares,
who goes the distance.

I dream of a nation
where people around the world
can come
to escape persecution and oppression,
to work with us
to build a better life.

We don't want the world's criminals.
But when good people
dream of a better life,
and come to our nation
to enrich us
with their dreams
and their work,
why wouldn't we
open the door?

How do we sort that out?
Isn't immigration
a lot like buying produce
at the grocery store?
Don't we want to keep the good apples
and return the bad?

I dream of a world
where there's no need for war
because people are so busy
helping one another
they don't have time
to kill each other.

Am I being naïve?
I don't know.

I do know that some people
are so fueled by hate
that they present a danger
to everyone around them.
I know sometimes
aggressors need to be stopped.

However,
while we deal with what is,
let's not forget
what could be.

I dream of a world
where there's no need to fight
about abortion
because the circumstances
that give rise to abortion
no longer exist.

I dream of a world
where women
in unplanned pregnancies
are respected,
listened to,
and understood,
instead of becoming pawns
in a political fight.

I dream of a world
where there's no need for unions
because companies compete
to outdo each other
in taking care of their employees.

Values

Do we all share the same values?
No.
But we can seek to understand
our collected values
whether we share each one
or not.

What are some of the values
that shape your views?

Here's one of my values:
History matters.

The past informs us.
The Holocaust,
the Soviet Gulag,
American Slavery,
and other tragedies of history
will show us
where danger lies
if we let them.

What went wrong in Nazi Germany,
Stalinist Russia,
the pre-Civil War South?
How did such oppression come about?
What can we learn to protect ourselves
and the nation we love?

Take the Holocaust,
for example.
In my view,
the people of Israel
have paid dearly
for the right
to enjoy their homeland
unmolested.

I want America
to defend that right.

Antisemitism,
is a cancer that will destroy
a people.

There are some things
that government cannot do.

For instance,
when an entire culture
is built around hate,
peace without oppression
is not possible.

Rebuild the culture
and peace will follow.
You can't do that
by changing the government.
You can only rebuild the culture
by changing how people think.

The earth is our home.
It looks like we'll be living here
for a long, long time.
So why wouldn't we
want to take good care of it?

Sooner or later,
every family has to come up with a plan
to get out of debt.

Why shouldn't our government
do the same?

Josef Stalin said,
"The people who *cast* the votes
decide nothing.
The people who *count* the votes
decide everything."

That's scary.
Election fraud
hurts everyone.

Thoughts

Conflict sells.
Without winners and losers,
there would be no NFL,
no NBA,
no professional sports of any kind.
Ask any novelist:
No conflict means no story.
So it's no wonder
the media focuses its spotlight on conflict.
The question is:
Do we want to play the media's game?
Just because the media
focuses on conflict
does that mean we must?

Keep in mind
that every member of the media
also steps into the voting booth.
That means
they have opinions
that cloud
everything they say.
The only truly objective person
is God Himself.

Suppose politicians
had to draft their legislation
before they were elected,
and it became law
the day they were sworn in.

Members of the media,
religious leaders,
teachers and university professors,
parents,
elected
and non-elected government officials,
business leaders,
labor leaders—
all of these people
have power and influence.
In each category
there are good people
and evil people,
and mostly people in between—
people who may mean well,
but sometimes let self interest
cloud their judgment.

Some believe that corporations are evil,
and some believe that government is evil.
I have news for you.
There's plenty of evil to go around
in both.
But there is also good in both.

Keep in mind,
however,
that there's one basic difference
between a corporation
and the government.
You can't boycott the government.

Government bureaucrats,
rich corporate CEOs,
union bosses,
church leaders,
and the list goes on—
all of these people
have a certain amount of power.
There are good people
and bad people
in all of these roles.
Corporations are not automatically good,
and unions are not automatically evil.
Nor is the opposite true.
Mostly all of these roles
are occupied by people
who sometimes get it right,
and sometimes get it wrong.

This is very important
to understand,
because much of politics
is about shifting power
from one group to another.

We can fight all day long,
for example,
on whether unions
should have more power
or corporations should have more power.
But how does that help us?
What really matters
is how the people who have power
are using their power.
Let's not assume that union leaders
or business owners
always have good motives.
Sometimes they do.
Sometimes they don't.

Shifting power
by itself
accomplishes nothing.
It may just mean
that powerless people
are oppressed by someone different,
and that's not a good thing.

I don't think any of us want
a sick or injured person
to go untreated.
Nor do we want
anyone to go bankrupt
because of medical bills.
Health care is a great problem to fix,
but look what happens
when we try to fix it the wrong way.
When people feel
that something is being shoved
down their throats,
what do they do?
Lots of anger.
Not much trust.
And instead of a solution
we can all embrace,
we have a protracted
political war
on our hands.

Health care,
like every other issue,
belongs to the people,
not to a political party.
Let's empower the people
to solve the problem.

One way to do this
is to test many different solutions
all over the country.
Embrace the ones that work.
Drop the ones that don't.
When 80-85% of the country
supports a tested group of solutions,
then we make it national policy,
but not until.
And we always keep the door open
to creative alternatives,
to new innovation
that may promise to solve the problem
even better for the next generation.

What business
does the government have
defining marriage?

Just asking.

The purpose of government
is to allow good people
to do whatever they want,
and to keep evil people
from getting in the way of that.

In an ideal world,
our need for government
would be greatly diminished.
We wouldn't need a military,
because there would be no threat of war.
We wouldn't need police or prisons
because there would be no crime,
no traffic accidents.
We wouldn't need welfare
because there would be no poverty.
We wouldn't need
environmental protection
or consumer protection.
All the power
would be given back to the people
because the people would use
that power only for good.
Every day then,
let's do something
to make this an ideal world,
so we can give the power
back to the people.

Don't underestimate the value of freedom.
Governments can and do
torture and murder dissidents.
What is a dissident?
If you think for yourself,
and have the courage to say
what you believe,
you are a dissident.
There is a government somewhere
that would like to see you dead.
If you're not careful who you vote for,
that government could be your own.

You never go wrong
being kind to somebody in need.
One thing that makes America great
is our generosity.
We help people
all over the world.
Sometimes that comes
in the form of government aid.
But more often
it's individual American families
sacrificially sending a gift each month
to help a child in need.

Who says there isn't any good news
out there?

A little kindness goes a long way.

The pie grows as we grow.
Let's not think
that the only way
to get money for ourselves
is to take it away from someone else.
Instead, let's all think
about what we can give,
what we can add,
what we can contribute.
And let's remember that money
is not the only thing that has value.

Always remember to read
between the lines.
Simply because
something has a pretty name,
doesn't mean
that we want it.

For example,
the United Nations
Convention of the Rights of the Child
(CRC treaty),
sounds nice, right?
But is it really about rights for children?
Or is it about something else
like taking away
rights for parents
and authorizing the persecution
of families
that don't fit
some bureaucrat's concept
of what a family should be?
Do we really want a treaty
that would override all American laws?
Do we we really want
people outside the United States
issuing interpretations
binding on all Americans?

We do our research
when we see something like this.
And when we read
of nightmare scenarios
where children
are taken away from their parents
for no good reason
where this treaty is in force,
we ask ourselves the question:
Do we really want it here?

Don't think that power like this
won't be abused.
It will,
and the next victim
just might be you.

As you think through
where you stand
on different issues,
ask yourself,
"What is everyone assuming?
And do I want to assume
the same thing?"

Let me give you an example.
On June 25, 1962,
the US Supreme Court
decided that teachers
and other school officials
could not lead students in prayer.
This decision divided the nation
into two groups:
those who wanted prayer
returned to the classroom,
and those who rejoiced
because it was taken out.

The Court
looked to the First Amendment
of the US Constitution:
"Congress shall make no law
respecting an establishment of religion,
or prohibiting the free exercise thereof
..."

So here's my quiz question for you:
What was the Court assuming?

Can you figure it out?

The court assumed

because the government pays for education,

that education

is an extension of the government.

Therefore,

teachers and other school officials

are acting as agents of the government

when they carry out their duties.

Do you see a problem with that?

I do.
Let's use that reasoning:
The government pays for health care.
Now hospitals
are an extension of the government.
So you may no longer have prayer
in hospitals,
even if a patient is dying
and begs a chaplain to pray.
The government pays for food stamps.
Now meals
are an extension of the government.
You may no longer pray at meal time.

Suppose we challenge
the Court's assumption.
What if education
was not an extension of the government
at all?
What if it was really
an extension of the family?
What if the government's only role
in education
was to empower families
to educate their children?

What if parents
made the final decision
about how their children
are to be educated?
What if parents decided
whether they wanted prayer—
or anything else—
for their children or not?

Let's look at it another way.
Suppose you're at the grocery store.
You go through the aisles,
make your selections,
come up to the register,
and get ready to check out.
But the store manager
walks up,
overturns your cart,
and informs you
that you don't know how to buy groceries.
Instead,
he must pick out groceries for you
because he knows more about groceries
than you do.
How would that kind of
"smarter-than-thou" attitude
make you feel?

When families,
particularly poor families,
minority families,
inner city families,
are robbed of the power
to choose their children's education,
they feel the same way
only worse.

Many of our teachers
are wonderful,
dedicated,
caring human beings
who deserve every penny
they're being paid
and much, much more.

But top down control
of education
does not empower educators
to break free
of a 19th century model
that badly needs to be updated
to work in the 21st century.

What would happen
if we gave control of education
back to parents and families?
What if parents had the power
to find the school
that was best
for their children?

And why do we assume
that one size fits all?
Isn't everybody different?
Shouldn't different approaches
to education
be used for different people?

In Freshman English
we read William Golding's
Lord of the Flies.
It's a simple story.
English school boys
are stranded on an island
following a plane crash.
The pilot is dead;
the boys must fend for themselves.
Intoxicated with this power,
freedom
and responsibility,
the boys break into two armed camps
and set out to annihilate each other.
In process,
they nearly burn down their island,
sending up smoke
that alerts a passing Royal Navy ship.
Only when the ship's officer
stands on the shore
do they stop fighting
and remember who they are:
English school boys.

Let's dedicate ourselves
to that moment
when we stop fighting
and finally remember who we are—
human beings
who just want the best
for ourselves,
our families,
and one another.

Promises

If elected,
I promise
never to blame my predecessors
for the mess.
That won't even be on our radar,
because
as a nation
we'll be having so much fun
cleaning it up.

You won't see me
bad mouthing other candidates.
That's not who I am.
You and I can learn something
from each of them,
because that's who we are.

I hope to be the first
presidential candidate
in the history of the United States
to run against myself
in the general election.
You read that right:
I hope to get both
the Republican and
the Democratic
nomination for president.

That won't be easy.
We have a lot of work to do.
Laws need to be changed.
Hearts need to be changed.
But together we can do it.

One thing you can count on is this:
I will never call you and ask
for a cent of your money.
I'm not that kind of person.
No,
this is a grassroots campaign
that will be won or lost
by ordinary people
spreading the word,
sharing with their friends
a new kind of hope
for America.

You won't find me
at the end of any leash
held by a lobbyist;
I chart my own course.
I can't be bought
by any special interest group
because I will NOT accept
even one cent of PAC money.
I'm the candidate of the people,
and I go way, way beyond
this Democrat-Republican squabble.
A vote for Dove is a vote for you.
You're in charge of my campaign,
and I'll put you
in charge of America.

Your power starts here…
DoveforPresident.com
Share the Dove for President message
with political candidates
or anyone else
by sending a copy of this book.
We do all the work for you;
all you do is tap or click.

About Dove

Due to the large number of
marriage proposals,
campaign contributions,
and write-in votes
she has received,
Dove Fogico
feels compelled to tell you
she is 100% fictitious (make believe). She
does not exist.
Really.
Dove Fogico lives on South Street
in Sun Prairie, Wisconsin, USA.
She drinks raspberry iced tea.
She has been seen in the company of
Straight Arrow aka Doug Johnson.
She has been to the Kingdom of Arken
three times.
She is running for president.
And you might want to unscramble
the letters of her name.
Find out more about Dove
in *The Man from Sun Prairie*.
https://goo.gl/nj7DyV or
http://goo.gl/9bvWHC (Amazon)

The Man from
Sun Prairie

Dwight Clough

Join the movement!
Dove for President
bumper stickers
yard signs
hoodies
t-shirts
mugs
bags
cases
and much more
for women, men and kids at
cafepress.com/doveforpresident

Dove for President
on Facebook
https://goo.gl/5s09eE

Your power starts here…
DoveforPresident.com
Share the *Dove for President* message
with political candidates
or anyone else
by sending a copy of this book.
We do all the work for you;
all you do is tap or click.